MOONSTRUCK!

by
Blodwen E. Jones

Copyright © 2020: Blodwen E. Jones

All rights reserved. No part of this publication may be produced, distributed, or transmitted in any form or by any means, including photocopying, recording, or other electronic or mechanical methods, without the prior written permission of the publisher, except in the case of brief quotations embodied in critical reviews and certain other non-commercial uses permitted by copyright law.

First Printed in the United Kingdom, 2020

Published by Conscious Dreams Publishing
www.consciousdreamspublishing.com

Edited by Daniella Blechner

Typeset by Oksana Kosovan

Cover designer: Rowenna Morag

The caricature: Morris Thompson

ISBN: 978-1-912551-93-4

SHUNKAHA

There's a loooong list of people who should be mentioned here [or maybe not], from birth to the present day. Family, friends, past, present and future. Even acquaintances etc. People who have helped, hindered, guided and chivvied me along my life path.

I haven't always appreciated my numerous and occasionally humorous lessons – as I have more often than not been in a darkly depressed place.

So to those of you still here on Mother Earth and those who are in Spirit, I give my heartfelt thanks for all that you have done to guide and help me on life's good Red Road.

MITAKUYE OYASIN

DEDICATION

This book is dedicated to all the maidens, mothers, crones, past, present and future all rolled into one.

I hope that what I have written will help you in some way to see that we are not alone. I feel that sharing my experiences with you, may show a way forward using your personal power.

Many of us have been on similar journeys, but haven't been able to talk about them.

Laughter is the best medicine. So laugh at the vagaries of life – when you can.

Love, light and healing to you all.

CONTENTS

Chapter 1. Satori

She Who Provides 12
Blue Moon 13
Little One 14
Earth 15
My Soul is Eternal 16
The Future 17
Jai Maadi 18
Two Great Laws 19

Chapter 2. Heterogeneous

Me! 22
Pussy Power! 23
Crime for Drugs – or Drugs for Crime? 24
Winter 26
Hope 27
Transmogrification 28
Automaton 29
Life 30
Remedy 31
Housework! 32
End-ing? 33
The White Stick! 34
Respect 35
Segs on my Bum 36
Virago 37

Termagant!	39
Unsheathed Claws	40
Lost	42
Give 'em Hell!	43
Woman	44
I Believe	45
Secrets & Ghosts	46
"A Gift"	47
My Mother …	48
A Lot of Old Flannel?	50
Laughter	51

Chapter 3. Poems Written From a Neurodiverse Perspective

Lunacy	54
Men & Us	55
Psychosis?	56
Naked!	58
Oh Shit!	59
Lunatics?	61
Tough Stuff	63
Trauma	64
Life!	66
Robotic?	67

Chapter 4. Damaged Goods

My Pledge	70
Lionel Richie	71

Men!	72
Me	73
Don't …	74
Incessant Demands	75
Misled	77
STD's	78
Key Collection	79
Thanks?	80
Really?	81
I'm Not Your Wife	82
Elsewhere	84
Clarity	85
Stay Strong	86
Literally	87
Selling Myself!	88
Fickle Lover	89
A Rock & A Hard Place	91
Sorted	93
What a Fucker!	94
Finally	95
Communication?	96
Well!	97
A Confession	98
Oh Yeah!	99
!!!	100
Bewitched	102
Oh No!	103
About the Author	**105**

CHAPTER 1

Satori

She Who Provides

I want to be a **free** citizen of the world,
humanity united under a common flag unfurled.
No more **discrimination** 'cos of the look upon your face,
just **acceptance** as a member of the human race.

If all are **truly** equal in the eyes of the great ONE,
then is there need for conflict before the day is done?
What need for many to starve, while others are well fed,
for some to live a life of charm, instead of one of dread?

What point in wars that wreck all of our lives,
leaving scars and pains to harm all that survives?
Look what we've done to our home – MOTHER EARTH,
a beautiful entity, who helped bring us to birth.

She freely provides us with all of our needs,
much of her bounty carrying their own seeds.
We have lost our respect for SHE who provides,
ignoring HER needs in our greedy, meteoric rise.

When will we put right this heinous wrong,
welcoming each day, acknowledging HER song?

Blue Moon

Angel of magic is healing for me
with power drawn from the moon and sea.
She reaches for a moon – oh so blue
full of potential for me and you.
Empowerment is what I asked for,
I feel she's opened that very door.

Little One

Tears in my eyes as I watch your birth,
welcome little one, to Mother Earth.
From the stars you came, to them you'll return,
and in-between times there's a lot to learn.
Many the people who will be your guide,
some will be true, most will have lied.
Remember Great Spirit and heed that call,
for it is the truest one of all.
Hear that truth spoken in your heart,
for it can't lie to you to set you apart.
Remember the lessons through the years,
as life's full of laughter, joy and tears.
Though pain and grief may cloud your sight,
recall the good times and set it right.
Find the balance in all that you do,
for the one true answer is found in you.

Earth

Past, present and future, all rolled into one,
this good Earth blessed by Grandfather Sun.
Time is out in the Grandmother's book,
Creations beauty deserves more than a look.
Great Mystery may hold that special key,
that led me to you and you to me.

My Soul is Eternal

I am ageless.
I am older than time.
I am here in female form.
My soul is eternal.

I am here to serve the source.
I have given birth to two truths.
I have lived through many deaths.
I have survived.

I am.
Me.
Alone.

The Future

Pink, grey and gold, colours that touch my soul –
in the ecstasy of a beautiful sunset.
Pain, hurt and sorrow, a reminder of tomorrow –
and what there might have been.

Anger, rejection and fear, hold me here –
facing my past alone.
Hope, faith, my truth – keep me aloof –
while I find my way back home.

Following a path that is often unseen –
finding a way that honours the dream.
Considering the others I'll pass on my way –
will they be with me at the end of the day?

What of the future, the chances of peace,
and goodwill to all life – not just mankind?
What left for our children's children –
death and decay – or life for the living –
each moment – every day?

Jai Maadi

"No problem", Jai Maadi said to me –
"Now write me a poem quite soon"
The trouble with people like him you see,
is they get you to dance to their tune.

~ooo~

Watching your smile come out to play –
like a ray of sunshine on a cloudy day –
gladdens my heart with that beam of light –
showing the GODDESS in you is right.

Knowing the words you speak are true,
as you look at life from a different view.
Honouring within, as well as without –
of your saintliness I have no doubt.

Trusting the windows to your soul –
I know you aren't just playing a role.
You're special, caring for many and not one
would deny you shine like the moon and the sun.

Two Great Laws

Now you're on the path, aiming for the light,
anything is possible, if it's done for right.
If you soar like eagle in the light of day,
Spirit will guide you to a better way.
Bat emerging into night can bring rebirth,
if you remember you're part of Mother Earth.
Spiders' web can show you the grand plan,
a connection with everything, even woman and man.
Crows caw will remind you of the two great laws,
of living in harmony, united in our cause.

CHAPTER 2

Heterogeneous

Me!

66 years old and **finally** coming into my power!
Why did it wait to happen 'til this late hour?
Where did all the hopes and dreams go?
Why has my learning been so slow?

Life has passed by in a weird way –
now here I am at the start of a new day.
I'm looking at making a fresh start –
by sharing experiences from the heart.

I hope that my poems will show others how –
we are not alone in the here and now.
So many of us have had a similar feeling,
of painful times that have left us reeling.

Take heart in the knowledge you're not alone.
I hope by reading this book you will be shown
that you need to talk to someone you trust,
as the devil drives when needs must.

Most of my life I've been as miserable as sin –
how to explain that – where do I begin?
Perhaps you'll get a sense of how it's been –
if you reach the last page, you may see what I mean.

Pussy Power!

Anyone who has one, knows just what it's like,
to have to give it a regular loving brush!
Mine is very difficult to get to, in oh so many ways.
and I want to get on with it as I am always in a rush.
He's such a little darling when he wants to be,
but more often than not, he's a cat,
who occasionally gets on my lap.
Who'd have thought I'd get to that.
'Cos when I got him he was a little sod,
he tore up my bedroom net curtain,
it was hanging there in shreds!
Whether to keep him or not I wasn't certain.
I cried, I moaned, I gritted my teeth,
and kept plodding on, having patched the threads.
He's at the door now when I get back,
and puts his paw around it. Be careful where I tread!
He's got a lot wrong with him and is an up-chucker,
practically all I have, he has to claw.
But I do love the little fucker.

Crime for Drugs – or Drugs for Crime?

Early hours – fast asleep.
Phone is ringing – won't it keep?
Bleary eyed – climb out of bed,
to stop the clamour in my head.

Could be trouble – may be fine,
could be a hoaxer on the line.
Lift receiver – say "hello",
trouble calling – have to go.

When I get there – he looks high,
is it worth it? Give it a try.
Once again – go through procedure,
he's your son – and needs yer!

Crime for drugs – or drugs for crime?
Will he end up doing time?
Locked in a prison – of whose making?
Is it JUST the drugs he's taking?

Will he live – or will he die?
Will he notice how I cry,
for the life – he's left aside,
and the self he's long denied?

I'm his mother – can't he see,
what he really means to me?
I gave life – I will not take it,
unconditional – love must fit.

Well, at last – he's got it licked,
after many times of being nicked.
He's settled down – with his lover,
and I'm soon to be a grandmother.

Winter

Each night I lie here wondering,
when there might be signs of spring?
I patiently await the first thaw,
but winter looks to last for evermore!

'Tho summer's heat a killer can be,
it would be better than this misery,
of waiting for my heart to soar,
and my soul to sing for evermore!

Hope

Life's a bitch – don't let it get to you,
helps you to understand what's right and true.
Lessons galore – you keep on learning,
while the wheels of time keep turning.

Good times are few and far between,
but keep you aiming for what's unseen.
Hope is what life's all about,
of that I feel there is no doubt.

So don't give up and don't give in,
to fake a life must be a sin.

Transmogrification

The person I am now bears no relation
to the woman who often went on vacation.
I've come into my own in some regard,
but the journey to date has been so hard.

Things are looking up I have to say,
the old maxim being – every dog has its day.
Well I'm having mine and loving it too,
and I've stopped some pills 'cos I ain't so blue.

Automaton

Sick of feeling like this,
someone up there's taking piss.
My pound of flesh came AFTER birth,
leaving me stranded, here on earth.

I'd have picked a life of bliss,
I didn't ask for **any** of this.
ME, I'm on a losing ticket,
from **first** breath I'd fluffed it.

Wrong life, era, planet, universe,
maybe I'm the mummies' curse!?
I mean, why me do you think,
have I **ever** raised a stink?

I've done my best trying to conform,
no-one said I'd have to perform.
You love this and care for that,
what do they take me for – a prat?

It took some time to realise,
what's been in front of their eyes.
An automaton can't say no.
I'm re-programmed, raring to go.

Life

I wish my life could flow,
like the river heading for the sea.
All obstacles in my path overcome quite easily.

I want to review my life from a great height,
like a soaring bird enjoying the freedom of flight.
To spend some time watching the world go by,
with no problems at all in my mind's eye.

Remedy

Tears of what – waiting to be shed,
along with this feeling heavier than lead?
How can I find the remedy for a cure,
when nothing in life is certain sure?

I don't even know the cause of this,
let alone transform it to a state of bliss.
All I can do is hope and pray,
that one day the feeling will fade away.

Housework!

Time on my hands for doing what?
Without some readies – not a lot.
How often did I used to say,
"If only I had time – maybe one day?"

Well now I've got it and not a clue,
of the million and one things I wanted to do.
There's plenty that needs doing – that's for sure,
but I don't enjoy housework any more.

Being married to a house is bad for us women,
doing a life-sentence serving men.
[Fathers, brothers, sons and lovers],
I'll tell you one thing – without a doubt,
it's years of housework that's worn me out!

End-ing?

Why do the key tasks in housework end in …ing?
Cooking, cleaning, shopping, washing, ironing, hoovering,
to name but a few that is.
I could list more, but I don't want to be seen as an incorrigible bore.

Isn't it funny how you think of these things,
or is it just me and my odd imaginings?
Then again – it's hardly surprising I've come to this,
after years of cleaning up – after others taking the piss.

So now I'm sitting here and time's worn me out,
and hit me full force with a heck of a clout.
My senses are reeling from the shock of the blow,
will I recover? I really don't know.

The White Stick!

My friend Jan,
takes the **greatest** pleasure in reminding me,
whenever she can,
of when I stood on the stick of a guy who couldn't see!
We were in my local store,
she opened her mouth and **very** loudly,
in a voice that was hard to ignore,
declared quite proudly,
"Trust you Blod, it's not as if it was invisible".

I often question if I can be seen,
as people wander around in a dream.
Having said that,
I felt a right prat
when I nearly sent a nun flying!
I wasn't even trying.
I don't know how it occurred,
but you have my word,
that before I knew it,
my walking stick
had landed on the back of her shoe.
Admitting it's been hard, but true.

Respect

I want to be a hermit residing in a cave,
nobody around to hear me – should I choose to rant and rave.
I want to be sufficient – unto no-one but myself.
No more pretence of anything, just taking care of my health.

I'd want to keep in touch with those of a like mind,
who take me as they see me – no matter **what** they find.
As for those who use me and often suck me dry,
then leave me alone and wondering why I bother to try.
I'd leave them 'til I'm ready to face their constant demands,
but until then I'd have to say, of them I'd wash my hands.

But reality's so different from my need for time for me,
so many people around, just don't have eyes to see,
nor ears to hear my protests when too much they expect
of my limited resources – whatever happened to respect?

Segs on my Bum

Unable to work in an acceptable way,
"What's wrong with her?" I hear people say.
"No visible signs to label her ills,
it's all in the mind, just give her some pills."

If we could swap places for five minutes or ten,
you'd be more than happy to change back again.
Knowing my life has come to this,
you'd consider yours as one of bliss.

Pain so intense, I can't get anything done,
I just have to sit here getting segs on my bum!
Frustration at wanting to get on with life,
instead, I'm left coping with all of this strife.

This is the way I'm feeling today,
worse than I was just yesterday.
Tomorrow it could be different again,
but I'll deal with that, as and when.

Virago

How can someone tell you that they are your friend,
then do their best to try to send you round the bend?
This has happened to me before,
but this time too, is hard to ignore.
Last time, I was sectioned and they wouldn't let me out,
she knows all that and there's no doubt,
she used that knowledge to play her game,
of mental torture. Am I to blame?
I ignored the obvious signs on show,
and hoped that all her angst would go.
Instead it got worse until
she came around and got her way.
She talked at me for ages
and when I said "**Enough**" flew into one of her rages.
I asked her to leave, but she refused to go,
and started acting out, her favourite show.
Before I knew it she attacked me quickly,
putting the blame on me so slickly!
She accused me of going for her,
which in fact was a huge slur.
Later that day I was asked what had happened to my lip.
I hadn't even noticed it was split when I took a sip
of the tea I'd made myself when she'd gone!

I was surprised that my nose hadn't shone
where she hit it! It didn't even bleed!
Some friend she turned out to be indeed.
So now I have to do my best to get over it,
and not let anyone else treat me like shit.

Termagant!

Sent from hell,
to put me under a spell?
You turned out to be a right royal bitch,
or are you just needing to scratch your itch?

What the **fuck** was that all about?
Why did you need to scream and shout?
I thought that the police would be called,
as that was how loud you **screamed and bawled**!

You ain't welcome here anymore.
If you turn up I won't open the door.
See you in the street, I'll cross over,
I'm tired of you. You are a drover.

Unsheathed Claws

Dragon fell from the darkening sky,
her wings all tattered and torn.
She landed in a field nearby,
and sat looking extremely forlorn.

She contemplated her awful state,
then turned with a baleful eye,
to regard what became her fate,
when she'd mated with the wrong guy!

At first it had been a huge relief
when he'd moved in to share her trough,
so she found it beyond belief
that her mate could have turned so rough.

They'd met on a starry, moonlit night,
introduced by mutual friends,
who'd convinced her that he was alright.
Had they known of his violent trends?

When first his unsheathed claws came out,
she had thought it an accident,
but then he'd fetched her an awful clout
and she realised it had been meant.

Considering things now, with hindsight,
she saw what a fool she had been
to suffer such a desperate plight
instead of following her dream.

She felt that she had lost so much.
her love, her home, her respect for self,
but especially that loving touch
that stopped her being left on the shelf.

Now she could look with cloudless eyes
at events from a new direction
and this helped her to realise,
she must provide her own protection.

She knew that she mustn't return to him,
that she needed to be much stronger.
Her chances of survival had grown quite slim
and death wouldn't be much longer.

She knew she was lucky to be alive
and blessed the powers that be,
for giving her the strength to survive
and relate to us – her sad story.

Lost

Sitting here, hiding my presence from you,
having told them you don't have a clue.
I didn't want to betray your trust,
but considering circumstance felt I must.

You looked so lost when he gave you the news
that you'd have to stay, you couldn't choose.
No more hiding the truth of your health,
fooling them with your lies and stealth.

Give 'em Hell!

My nain [North Wales Welsh for grandmother] was an old bag,
she really was you know.
But one thing I did tell her
was, "I do love you, you know".

There were times she caused such ructions within the family,
but you know the old bag meant all the world to me.
She introduced me to the world of books, and not just me you know.
Her love of literature provided a warm and inner glow.

She shared her world of escapism from the reality in which we live,
sadly, that was all she was ever truly able to give.
Everyone who knew her has an anecdote to tell
of her being a real character who enjoyed giving others hell!

Woman

I feel like an unloved, unwanted gift in a charity shop.
People pick me up, and put me down in disgust.
Why do I get treated like the bad apple in the crop,
when all I want is someone who I can love and trust!

"Is it really me?" I ask myself
"What did I do to end up on this old, dusty shelf?
Perhaps one day I WILL meet Mr. Right,
who might stay with me for the occasional night.

In the meantime I must get on with life
and do what I can to improve the strife,
of not knowing if I'm doing anything wrong.
"Come on woman. You have to be strong."

I Believe

Don't let old age sneak up on you
without having lived your life.
Try to see things from a different view
to deal with all the stress and strife.
Before you know it you'll be looking back
and wondering **"Where the hell did 16 go?"**
If things ain't working out, try a different tack.
Move in a new direction and you will grow.
Take what life is offering as you go along.
I know it's not easy to trust in the great plan,
but you've just got to go for it, try to be strong.
Somehow I have done it and I believe you can.

Secrets & Ghosts

Child inside knows the truth; adult has locked her away.
As she grows, her body knows, its reactions holding sway.

Logical adult looks around and questions what may be,
the child inside now chooses to hide from the woman who is me.

My mind says YES; my body NO; when will they unite?
Will my spirit find the way, when it returns from its desperate flight?

My heart says YES, my head says NO; my life is in a whirl,
what happened in the distant past, to that little lonely girl?

I want to take her by the hand and lead her away from the pain,
to find with her the joy in life, to laugh and love again.

I hope that she will come to see that we are really one,
when she can share her secrets with me, all our ghosts will be gone.

"A Gift"

My father took me by the hand and led me down the stair,
he signalled silence for what we two, alone would share.
He led me to the sofa and pulled me on his knee,
"Remember now, a secret this, just for you and me."

His hands began a wandering, creating urges anew,
something special, just for me. "A gift," he'd said, "for you."
I closed my eyes in pleasure, trusting his loving touch,
writhing beneath the fingers that excited me so much.

His breathing grew more ragged as his penis became hard,
he raised my nightie, opened my legs and then he marked my card.

My Mother ...

disempowered me in oh so many ways,
and I doubt I can forgive her by my end of days.
She treated me as of no consequence,
looking back her attitude makes no sense.
Her use of me knew no bounds,
it was even worse than it sounds.

Physical, mental and emotional abuse,
of my Spiritual too she made misuse.
She left the sexual side of it to my dad,
that was the only loving I ever had.
I was the eldest of her brood of five,
only three of us are left alive.

I had to go to town and pay the bills
and to the village to get her pills.
Shop, cook, clean, look after HER children,
do my homework, go to school and then
do well in all they had to teach.
Her sense of reality was out of reach.

Trust me when I say
nothing I did was good enough, no way.
I eloped aged seventeen
to get away from her obscene treatment of me.

Many years later when she died,
I have to be honest, I never even cried.
She'd continued to fuck up my life
and do anything she could to create strife.

But I feel the worst thing she ever did for me
was back my ex to take my kids away, you see.
He wasn't even their dad.
Shows you she was really bad.

I don't know why I'm relaying all this,
maybe your life's not been one of bliss.
I hope that this will help to show
that the travails of life help us to grow.

A Lot of Old Flannel?

I want to write something funny.
I need to have a laugh.
Maybe I should think about it when I'm having my bath!

I wonder if the bubbles will go up my nose?
Or if I'll pull the plug out, accidentally with my toes?
Perhaps the flannel will fall apart after all the years of use
or am I being just a little bit obtuse?

Today is not a day for laughter, or so it seems.
Instead it would appear to be all about following my dreams!

Laughter

The Comedy School is a **brilliant** concept
which has made me at least, more adept
at using my humour in a positive way.
That **can't** be bad at the end of the day.

The IMPROV course I went to,
was set up with SLaM's recovery college, it's true!
The seven week course passed by so quick,
the three facilitators were **really** slick.

I haven't laughed so much in the past before
and I hope to go on laughing a lot more.
It also helped to build up my confidence,
and showed me how to be less intense.

I had to have tissues to wipe my eyes,
as the tears of laughter were a big surprise!
Each session was a joy to attend
and I felt sad when it came to the end.

Long may it continue to deliver such joy
to all of the people who want to employ,
Keith and his talented team of funnies.
They're great comedians, not bunnies!

CHAPTER 3

Poems Written From a Neurodiverse Perspective

Lunacy

Moonstruck – afraid of going over the edge again?
Why is everything so weird, strange, magical and then
I realise it's the time of the great awakening
and it's a journey into the unknown I'm undertaking.

Madness isn't just a state of mind,
to call it lunacy is being very unkind.
It's the opening of a door between space and time,
where there's no reason, sense or rhyme.

I can now look back over what's happened to me
and see it's formed the person I've come to be.

Men & Us

I do empathise with men you know, as they don't have it easy either.
They are supposed to be the strong ones and were given a reminder.
"Big boys don't cry. Man up. Don't be a pansy. You're a wuss.
What are you going on about, what's all this fuss?"

For them to **talk** about their feelings is **not** on their agenda.
Instead they often cover them up by going on a bender.
It isn't just a man thing, women struggle too.
'Cos admitting to any weakness isn't seen as good for you.

We all need to open up our channels of communication,
as hiding our hurts and fears causes retaliation.
We all react to what's happened in our past,
no matter what we think or say. I feel it's time at last,
to put everything into perspective.
We need to make the time to be more reflective,
so we can all move on in life
and make an end to all the strife.

Psychosis?

I don't have a telly and people wonder why.
Now let me tell you something and I don't have to lie.
They say "I don't blame you. There's nothing to see
and I would get rid of mine if it was down to me."
But I got rid of mine for reasons you mightn't understand,
at times the way it talked to me was **very** underhand.

I once sat here writing the show that was on the screen,
my family all around me doing their best to be serene.
I was away again with the fairies – having been there before,
my **off the wall** behaviour must have been hard to ignore.

Was that the time I followed space ships moving through the sky
and cars turning left or right as they were passing by?
I think this was the first time and I didn't have a crowd.
I'd ended up on a street corner, shouting and swearing out loud.

"A vicar approached me and asked "Are you alright?"
His unexpected appearance gave me **such** a fright.
My partner appeared soon after, as he'd been looking for me.
He asked the vicar to take me home and gave to him the key.

He was off to find my son, who was also out to search
For a woman who had lost her way and left them in the lurch.
The vicar saw me to the door, but refused a cup of tea.
To be quite honest, I think he was afraid of me.
To be fair to him, he'd seen me home and let me in my door.
Then off he went and I recall no more.

Naked!

Rocking in the mad house, with little else to do,
'cept keep the beat 'tween taking pills – remember not to chew.
Swallow the medicine to keep your cool,
it's dancing through you – but you're nobody's fool.

Waiting for others to provide the drink and food
in **their** own good time – IF you're awake and shrewd.
Enough awareness left to realise
just who's the Prince of Deception & Lies.

Watching the marks fade from that last beating
where you were dragged off the floor kicking and screaming!??
KICKING & SCREAMING?

Naked, sweating – a Spiritual cleansing, changed,
to cuffed, pinioned by the 'Lords of the Dance', deranged
by their powers – endowed by the false gods of these times.

Oh Shit!

Suicidal thoughts are bouncing 'round my head again.
"Kill yourself, just kill yourself," say the voices in my head!
"Go on – do it. You'd be better off dead."
How can I begin to explain how I feel when
this happens day in and day out?
It's a bloody nightmare, there's no doubt.
People think it's easy to deal with all the shit
of living with mental illness "Just get on with it."

"Pull yourself together," people often say;
I wonder how they'd cope at the end of the day?
I'm sick of all their platitudes.
We need to change the attitudes
of oh so many people to mental health.
Looking at the stigma and stealth
of how it just creeps up on you.
A review of it all is long overdue.
There are no words to explain it.
You feel like you're in a deep pit
and there's no way out.

You daren't scream or shout
'cos that way leads to sectioning.
Then there's no way to be moving

in a new direction for ages.
We have to hold on to the rages.
coursing through us each and every day.
You'd swap places with me? No way.

Lunatics?

I'm not looking to get pissed
and it ain't on my bucket list
of things to do before I snuff it.
I really want to improve the shit
of mental health provision
and making it fit for purpose is my vision.
It's the 21st Century,
decency is elementary
for goodness sake.
We are human beings, give us a break.
Stop treating us so condescendingly.
It could be you, it just happened to be me!
I didn't expect that I'd lose my mind,
not once but **five times**! Be kind
to those of us who are the one in four.

Please! Treat us decently and don't ignore
the fact that many of us have the capacity
of the world in a different way to see.
Ours is a very difficult path to travel,
never knowing if our minds will unravel,
leading us into an acute ward.
People seem to think we're a fraud.
I doubt very much you'd want to be us.

Stop treating our conditions and fuss
about the risk you think we present
to you and yours. Don't resent
that some of us are really unable to work
and we did have a life before and didn't shirk
our responsibilities. We did not ask for any of this
to happen to us. Get over us and **don't** take the piss.

Tough Stuff

Why am I in such a depressed mood?
Is it because last night you eschewed
my simple request for a hug?
Or is it really a case of having the bug
about the fact that childhood trauma has raised its head yet again?

Every time I think I have dealt with it, then
someone mentions the fact that it affects all your life.
No wonder I've had to deal with so much strife!
I have reached a point where I have had enough
of dealing with **a lot** of tough stuff.

The only consolation I can find
is that I **don't** intend to lose my mind
yet again. I have been OK-ish for twenty years
and losing touch with reality is one of my biggest fears.

I have learnt to put it down to experience
and that for me makes so much sense.
It means that I can use what I have been through
to help others have a different view
of mental health from my perspective.
Perhaps it will help them to be more effective
in providing a service fit for purpose.

Trauma

Will no one **ever** understand just **who** I really am?
The woman who's been damaged from birth, by what was done to harm.
A childhood so **full** of abuse, it doesn't bear thinking about,
if you heard just a snippet of it, I have no doubt you'd be shocked to the core.
It's continued throughout my life, need I say any more?

OK! I'll dig deep and open up the wounds to help you to understand,
the fact is that my parents were **very** underhand.
The outside world perceived them as good and decent folk,
who went out of the way to help others even when they were broke!

The only love my father gave me, was through sexual abuse!
As far as my mother was concerned, I was there for her misuse.
As soon as I was old enough she used me as her skivvy,
to do all that she demanded.
I had no choice but to do what she commanded.

At the age of 15, I tried to end it all
and the psychiatrist made the only call,
that my churchgoing days were done.
He'd agreed with her in all she said 'cept that one.

It's taken many years to realise why my life's been such a difficult journey,
but now I know if I'd had someone to hear ME really,
HEAR ME. Listen to the clues that are there.
Give me the time and space to be open and air
what's buried so deep inside my heart.
Allow me the chance to make a start
on healing the wounds that have marred my life
so I can begin to end the strife.

Life!

I need a poem I said to myself.
All this stress is affecting my health.
I want my life to be more serene,
to follow my heart and live the dream.

Love, joy and laughter to the end of my days,
to be just me in so many ways.
I want to be loved for being me,
not for what others expect me to be.

Some respect too wouldn't be a bad thing,
but hey! I want to get on with living.

Robotic?

Why do I find rejection so hard to take?
You'd think I'd be used to it by now for heaven's sake.
The pain doesn't seem to lessen, it just gets worse,
so I just want to scream really loud and curse.

But that wouldn't do, I'd be dragged away
and taken to the Maudsley for many a day.
Instead I'm up late lying in my bed,
with all these thoughts going 'round in my head.

I really hate feeling like this
when t'other person thinks nowt's amiss.
I need to sleep, or I may end up psychotic,
I feel I've been treated as though I'm robotic!

Chapter 4

Damaged Goods

[My experience of men – as a woman!]

My Pledge

Quality not quantity, is what I always say,
but when they come together, it really makes my day.
Your touch becomes harmonious with many of my needs,
then before I know it, I'm sprouting new seeds
of love and understanding – adding to the growth.
So, to improving standards, I pledge my troth.

Lionel Richie

Soft lights, seductive music, fishnet stockings and you didn't show!
I was tempted to throw on my mac, knock on your door and make you glow,
but I thought better of it and took them all off, placing them on the chair.
I then sat here thinking and drinking tea, listening to a voice oh so fair.

The words he was singing rang so very true, resonating with where I've been.
I know where you're coming from and I don't want to be seen as too keen.
It's just that you'd said you'd pop 'round for an hour or two,
I thought I'd surprise you with a different view.
I'd wanted to see the look on your face.
Oh well! Another time – same place?

 Men!

When it comes down to it, they're a breed apart.
Some with narcissistic tendencies will often break your heart.
Add to the mix if they're also a sociopath who knows how to manipulate well,
you find yourself thinking **you're** crazy when THEY put YOU through hell.

Now. Make it a threesome of a different kind
and include psychopathic tendencies to **really** blow your mind.
YOU'LL end up thinking, **"Where did the goal posts go?"**
They keep on moving them around and don't bother to let you know.

They're **very** charismatic and get you into bed
and before you know it, start to fuck with your head.
So take heart and learn from my mistakes.
Trust your instincts for heaven's sakes.

Me

What makes you so special, oh high and mighty sir?
Is it because you are a him or better than any her?
What right have you to treat me so?
To you I've done no wrong
and I'm not like other women, singing a siren's song.

Instead, I showed you my **true self** and this is what I get,
when all I've ever asked you is PLEASE, show me some RESPECT.

Don't ...

Call yourself my friend.
You're just a has been, a once was.
Someone who was around because
I was convenient for satisfying your needs.
Did you have nowhere else to sow your seeds
all the times you made use of me?
No other women that were free for you to see?
Or should I be blunt and say for you to fuck?
I suppose me being available was your good luck
in a funny sort of way, for a while at least.
I believe I helped to satisfy the sexual beast in you.
I must have been/was so naïve
to listen to your bullshit and really believe
a lot of the crap that came out of your gob.
I have to say that you did a good job
of convincing me that you were my friend -
and that's where this verse I will have to end.

Incessant Demands

I've come through major challenges in life,
as a daughter, lover, friend, mother and wife.
[Clean the sink first I think.]
My creativity gets side-tracked with all I need to do.
Computers 'ain't got nothing compared to me and you.
[I need to do the dishes that are sitting in the sink, but I'm
far too tired to make the link.
They're on the worktop and the cooker
And on top of it all, I'm meant to be a good lover!].
All the knockbacks, hurt, anger and pain,
without them, no wisdom to gain.
[A Madonna, (a woman?) or you're a whore.]
Insults that are so hard to ignore.
"She's a nymphomaniac" I've heard people say.
"He's just sowing his wild oats at the end of the day."
"She's a single parent and not so good as a mother."
He went off with her best friend as her lover!
It wasn't the first time he'd played the field.
Did he **ever** understand she was often too tired to yield
to his incessant demands to get her into bed,
dressed up to suit his latest fantasy, then give him more than head?
Two kids he'd given her to **prove** he was a man,
And left **her** to bring 'em up, do the dishes, cleaning, shopping,

much more than was fair to expect of one.
He'd treated her as if she was immune to his sort of con.
Anyway, now she's got her sense of self back [did she every really have it?]
Now she's older, a bit wiser and getting on with life using her wit.
So take heart [maybe] from what I've learned in life [if you want to].
It's much too short for strife.

Misled

I was conditioned to believe that **housework** is the most important thing in life.
That to be fulfilled, you had to become a mother as someone's wife.
Then create the ideal, happy home,
so the man you married wouldn't want to roam.

He'd come home to slippers by the fire,
with you dressed up to feed his sexual desire.
The 2.5 kids would be tucked up in bed,
fast asleep having had a story read.

To them, daddy's a man who is only seen at weekends.
Occasionally he'll go and say "G'nite", it depends
on the mood he's in when he walks through the door.
He works hard to ensure that they aren't poor.

Mummy's the one who is always there,
she is the one who is taking care
of them, the house, the cat and the dog.
Is it any wonder she sleeps like a log
when day is done and it's time for rest?
She's spent her day doing her best.

STD's

My first husband, although a rotten git, gave me two children. **Fair enough**.
My second husband, a **very** pervy man, gave me trichomoniasis.
That was **really** rough!
The guy who lived with me for many years gave me genital warts.
The last fella I had sex with gave me genital herpes of course.
[I know the last two lines don't rhyme,
But use your imagination, give it time].

The bottom line is **don't** have sex if you want to avoid trouble.
Be careful if you go for it and try not to burst your bubble
of believing that **you** are safe from all sexual ills.
You could end up with a load of pills
to help you cope with the stress
of finding yourself in an **unhealthy mess**.

Key Collection

You don't have a bed post and appear to collect keys instead!
Maybe it's time for you to invest in a bed,
as the way you're going the bunch will weigh you down.
Can't be easy carrying them all 'round the town.

How do you remember what key is for each door?
Have any of them noticed, but perhaps they chose to ignore
the fact that only one key is needed for your lock.
So many more than that comes as quite a shock.

Are you showing off your conquests to each and every one -
or just to me, you son of a gun?

Thanks?

I know I've slagged you off in verse,
but your treatment of me was getting worse.
I had to get it off my chest
so I could lay my emotions down to rest.

I wanted to be your friend at least,
going back to the famine – and not the feast.
Once again I've given in to your charm,
hoping you would do me no more harm.

Where do you **really** want to go with me?
From where I stand it's hard to see.
I think it's time to make my stand,
as you are being **very** underhand.

You've pissed me off, no denying that.
Do you really think I'm a total twat?
It seems to me that you're just a prick,
Who thinks of only where you put your dick.

Well **thanks** for your lack of concern,
I hope one day that you will learn,
there's more to life than a good fuck.
In the mean time I wish you luck.

Really?

I can see so clearly, now that you've been round.
You didn't want to hear me is what I found.
You had an answer for all I tried to say,
so I kept trying to tell you that I no longer want to play.
You did your best to charm and beguile me,
but I had more sense than to let you see,
just how much you'd **really** hurt my dignity.

I have to move on now – it seems a pity,
'cos in so many ways I care about you
and that what there was, was new.
Love comes in many different guises,
but not everyone realises
'til it's far too late to be saved.

I'm Not Your Wife

You shat on me from a great height,
by often saying you'd return later that night.
You'd change your mind and not let me know
that you had no intention to even show.

You've kept me dangling on a short bit of rope,
now I've reached the point where there's no hope
of **ever** having even my basic needs met.
You'd make suggestions and then forget,
how you asked me for X and suggested Y.
How many more times did you expect me to try
to comply with your expectations of me
and the sort of woman you want me to be?

With my head you kept on messing,
with all the misuse and second guessing.
Well **fuck you mate**, I'm **not** your wife.
You made it clear that you have a life
that you're more than happy with as it stands.

Now here is the brunt. I wash my hands
of the you I've really come to know,
not the guy who presented a show.
You pretended to be someone you're not,

sucked me in and then forgot
that to keep me sweet you had to be nice
and you took no notice of all my advice.
So now you may guess that I am **very** miffed,
and just in case you don't get my drift,
I've had more than enough of your attitude,
the way you treat me is extremely rude.

Now the veil's been lifted **again** from my eyes,
and the only thing I am able to surmise,
is that what's going on now is more off than on,
and the way you've treated me is **such** a big con.
Your voice is saying one thing, your actions show another,
so I've decided that it just 'ain't worth the bother.
I am off to get on with my life
and avoid all this stress and strife.

Elsewhere

Fidelity is a dirty word where a lot of men are concerned.
I want my man to be true to me I've really just learned.
I know now what I want from a man,
but more often than not, I don't think they can
fulfil all of my needs
without planting their seeds elsewhere.

Clarity

Am I supposed to be grateful for the crumbs from his sexual table?
The way he's treated me, leaves me feeling very unstable.
The games he plays aren't nice at all,
and he's the one who is having a ball.

When I try to relate how it's making me feel,
he just can't see that for me it's a big deal!
So just where do I go to from here?
I hope that in time, all will become clear.

Stay Strong

I need to find a way out of this unhealthy mess,
that's caused me untold and major distress.
I find it offensive to say the least
the way he raised the sexual beast
on his return from a long absence.
His attitude just makes no sense.

I mustn't go down that road again,
I need to stay strong when,
he comes back to look for sex.
I must avoid his touch 'cos of my reflex.
He knows just how to touch me and turn me on,
so I must avoid it and remember it's a con.

Literally

The fatted calf's been eaten,
all's left are the bare bones.
Now I'll not be beaten,
by all the undertones.
I have acted like a fool
in your game of chance,
I thought it was really cool
to enjoy a bit of romance.

The rose tinted glasses
already had a crack
and when I think of all the lasses
you've had on their back,
I wonder why I went there,
where's my sense of pride?
Truth to tell, I don't care,
I've just enjoyed the ride!
LITERALLY

Selling Myself!

No more sex for me when it comes at a price
of selling myself short. It's just not nice.
I refuse to take the line of easy way out,
then leave myself so full of doubt.

Again. Respect is what comes to mind
and that for me I have to find.
How can I expect men to give me some,
when all they want is to fuck and come?

Fickle Lover

It seems that recently I have become a "persona non grata" in your book.
Was it something I said? The way that I look?
Or just a case of you having better fish to fry?
Funny how you didn't even want to try
to make the effort to keep me sweet.
Well that's really cool and neat,
'cos guess what? I've had more than enough of your shit.
I am moving on, well away from it.
Don't come sniffing around looking to go there again.
I'm off in search of other men.
I am sure there's someone who will treat me right,
unlike the way you made me fight my conscience.
I'd already heard of your promiscuous ways
and still I got caught up in your dishonest gaze.

The bottom line is **you lied** my friend
and saying you are is the biggest one.
A friend is there for you when you are really ill,
they don't run and disappear for days on end.
They keep an eye on you 'til you're on the mend.
With you it's Sex, Sex and more Sex.
You never waver in your search for the latest flavour

of the day, night, week, month, year even!
You didn't get your way when I was ill, a good enough reason
I do believe, to tell you that your actions are a form of treason.

Well, I'm gonna share my dictum.
MEN! I've always messed up when I picked 'em.
Like it or not. I am out to find a man who would eschew
all of the things that make up you,
and I hope all your other women do too.
I hope you come to rue the day
you always had it all – your way.
That you find your perfect partner
And she responds with laughter
of disbelief at your cheek.
That you would believe she was weak
enough to drop her drawers
just so you could make her **yours**
until you got itchy feet again!
Is it just you or all men?

A Rock & A Hard Place

At long last I thought it was you at my door.
Then I heard my post drop to the floor!
Where the **hell** have you been hiding,
when I'm still here residing
in the place I've been for years?
I'm sitting here feeling close to tears!

What do you take me for – a moron
whose love of life is long gone?
I'll have you know that I am not a has been
but a woman who has often seen
more than was sometimes good for her.

Anyway. Did it **ever** really occur
to you that I have feelings
that you walk over leaving me reeling
from your onslaught?
I have been caught
between a rock and a hard place.

How do I get to save face
and walk well away
so I can live and love another day?

Sorted

You presented yourself as a well sussed out geezer.
Instead, you turned out to be a major pussy teaser.
You've picked me up and put me down,
then turned on the charm to change my frown
into something you wanted me to be.
A woman who is easy and free
with her sexual desires
once you have **stoked her fires**!

What a Fucker!

He is a callous bastard, who only thinks of one thing.
The way he carries on 'ain't healthy 'cos of the risks he did bring.
How can someone be so indifferent and not tell you just
what is at stake?
That's when you realise that in fact they're a terrible fake.

Trying to get in contact to resolve what is going on
has turned out to be impossible and proves they were always a con.
So I'm left with the horrible truth of it all,
he didn't give a damn and was having a ball!
So was I if I'm honest – in an odd sort of way –
but truth is he should have been honest too at the end of the day.

Finally

It's time for me to come clean
and tell you you're a has been.
You led me on a merry dance
but you've had your final chance.

I am moving on to pastures new
where I don't intend to include you
as the man who is a good shag.
You really believed I was in your bag.
Well, let me make it clear to you
that an end to this is well overdue.

Communication?

I talked to you 'till I was blue in the face
but you treated me as of non-human race.
I revealed my inner self – my true feelings,
but against that wall you kept on leaning.

I begged, I pleaded to be allowed inside,
but behind the armour – access denied.
Now it's a time for shedding tears,
after being together for so many years.

I have to stay, as you've chosen to go.
Good communication? I don't think so.

Well!

Fuck you! I thought you were my friend.
Your behaviour **almost** sent me 'round the bend!
Luckily I have cottoned on to you,
my time has come to have a review.

Of just where you are coming from? Well!
It seems you got me under your spell.
Now the veil's been lifted from my eyes
I can see so clearly – is that a surprise?

I know it's not been an easy ride,
but it's time for me to finally decide
just where I want to go with this
and put a stop to you taking the piss.

A Confession

To be honest, I have learned a lot from you.
You've helped me see another point of view.
I didn't think I'd look at some things the way I do now,
but you've talked to me without us having a row.
Your patience knows no end,
'tho to your will you tried me to bend!
Although you know me in so many ways
and for that I have to give you praise.

You will **never** know what I am capable of doing
and one of these days you may end up rueing
the way you have treated me with indifference.
I wish I had more than common sense,
but when it comes all the way down to it,
you're a thoughtless and selfish git.

Oh Yeah!

Well! It seems I've been unofficially dumped – who'd have thought it eh?
The way he played it for many a day
led me to believe that he'd always return.
Seems I still have a lot to learn.

They say "no news is good news", I guess it's true
'cos it's given me time to get over you.
I have my eye on some other guys
and I guess to my friends it's not a surprise.

They know I always bounce back up again,
especially when it comes to me and men.

Your sensual touch is my downfall.
Unfortunately I don't have the wherewithal
to avoid all your charms
and stay away from your arms.

My sensible head turns to mush
when your sweet talk gives me the push
you need to get me where you want.
Really and truly, I should find it an affront
to my dignity. I should tell you where to go.
Can I find the strength to do that. Don't think so!

But now I have the strength indeed
to tell you that I no longer need
to go there any more with you.
You've given me the ammunition – it's true
to tell you – if and when you get in touch –
that what you last gave me is too much.
I'm stuck with it now for the rest of my life!

Where are you now? Shagging someone else's wife?
Maybe that is the case, I don't know.
There are so many women for you to show
your "I'm a nice guy who does understand".
The way you behave is very underhand.

Bewitched

You sat there coming on to my friend,
and it wasn't the first time, with you it's a trend.
Were you just testing me out as I went off to put on the kettle?
I have to find the resolve and mettle
for keeping myself safe from your wiles and charm,
as you really don't see just how much you harm.
You prey on the vulnerable, old and sick.
Basically, any woman where you can stick your prick!
With you it's another one to add to the score,
to get all that you want, then walk out the door.

Having bewitched them by your charms and wiles,
your humourous words, great sex and smiles.
How many hearts have you broken along the way?
One day you'll find it's your turn to pay
when it's your teeth that are false
and your cock ain't so pert.
When the wrinkles are deep, then you will get hurt.
You'll fall head over heels for your perfect woman who
will show you what rejection feels like too.

Oh No!

One minute you're here and then **poof**! you're gone
and of the great sex – I ain't getting none.
But the signs are there that you are,
considering our chats – it's a step too far.

It's more than an attraction as I've come to realise,
More a case of – de ja vu. Is that in both our eyes?
You've said we are compatible – that's why you keep coming back.
But when I try to find out why, you lead me off my track!

I have to take responsibility for letting you take the piss
and giving in to your disarming ways as if there's nothing amiss.
Your honesty only goes as far as it suits your needs,
you use it to get your women and sow your very fertile seeds.

My fertility's in a different form these days.
It's running rampant in oh so many ways!
The poems are flowing thick and fast,
I'm making the most of it and hope it will **last**.

I have the title for my book and orders I didn't take down!
What the heck is wrong with me? Why am I acting like a clown?
What's happening now is magical and really intense.
If I didn't know better, it'd make absolutely no sense.

Onwards and upwards is what I'm saying.
If I was a wolf – at the full moon I'd be baying.
I have to be careful and aim to stay grounded.
By heck – is all that as bad as it sounded?

Anyway, my weird life has taken a different turn
and from all of its lessons I'm beginning to learn,
that "patience is a virtue" if you follow my bent
and often with me and my men it's been heaven sent.

So if there's a next man in my life, I hope I will get it right
'Cos I am sick of getting it wrong!
Now I've had enough of this verse. So **long**!

ABOUT THE AUTHOR

© Morris Thompson

Blod (as she prefers to be called) has a number of achievements under her belt which you may find interesting or boring!

She left school with no qualifications having made an attempt to leave the planet.

She has used the University of Life to her advantage where possible.

She eloped to Scotland and married at 17! Had her daughter exactly 8 months later and her son 15 months and a few days after that!

She spent many years as a single parent, trying to deal with everything under the influence of "Mother's little helper" – valium. What she really needed was some "Trauma Therapy".

She moved to London in 1980 with her 2 children, to live with longish term relationship number 3 of 5! (She is currently available for any interesting offers!)

She has a diploma in Counselling and Supervision, which she feels has helped her in many ways – although she can't find it at present!

Being sectioned 4 times was NOT on her bucket list, but it turned out to be the making of her.

She has a lot to thank SLaM (South London and Maudsley) for, especially in recent years. Having involvement with them through courses at the Recovery College and being on the Involvement Register, has helped her to re-invent herself as an "EXPERT BY EXPERIENCE AND WORDSMITH."

"Crime for drugs or drugs for crime?" was the first poem she kept. It was written in 1993.

Conscious Dreams
PUBLISHING

Be the author of your own destiny

Find out about our authors, events, services and how you too can get your book journey started.

- Conscious Dreams Publishing
- @DreamsConscious
- @consciousdreamspublishing
- Daniella Blechner
- www.consciousdreamspublishing.com
- info@consciousdreamspublishing.com

Let's connect

You may find some of the poems in here disturbing to say the least. [I did writing them!].
Profits from this book will go to:

- **Womankind**
- **MIND**
- **Alexander Paul Foundation**

www.ingramcontent.com/pod-product-compliance
Lightning Source LLC
Chambersburg PA
CBHW081352080526
44588CB00016B/2475